M000080680

KNOCK-OFF MONARCH

a collection of poems by
Crystal Stone

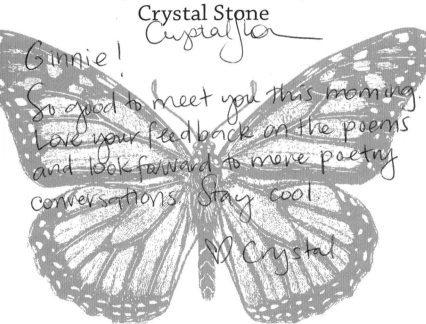

Ginnie!
So good to meet you this morning.
Love your feedback on the poems
and look forward to more poetry
conversations. Stay cool

♡ Crystal

DAWN VALLEY PRESS

Copyright © 2018 by Crystal Stone

All rights reserved. This book or any portion thereof may not be reproduced or used in any manner whatsoever without the express written permission of the publisher except for the use of brief quotations in a book review.

First Printing, 2018
Dawn Valley Press P.O. Box 112 Beaver, PA 15009
DawnValleyPress.com

ISBN-13: 978-0-936014-25-8

Library of Congress Control Number: 2018959975

Cover art: Erin Dakas
Cover design and layout: Michael Nyers, linkedin.com/in/michael-nyers-345455b1/

KNOCK-OFF MONARCH

a collection of poems by
Crystal Stone

TABLE OF CONTENTS

Acknowledgements 13

I.
First Impressions 17
On my drive home.. 18
Only 19
God is... 20
Against Faith 21

II.
Noah Goes to Rehab.. 25
Drawing Mother 26
Naming 27
In the Living Room 28
Nevertheless, Jochebed thought.................................... 29
Before the News 30
House Keys 31
Poverty... 32
One and Two Star Reviews of
Storybook Land, Egg Harbor Township, NJ 33
Kitchen 34
My Family as Disciples at the Last Supper 35
Mom Interrupts Solomon... 36
Ketoacidosis 37

III.
Promise.. 41
Vashti... 42
Bedroom 43
Describing Memory 44
Self-Portrait in Philadelphia 45
In the Grocery Store Parking Lot 46
Notes on an Afternoon Train 47
Surrender... 48
Transformation 49
Self-Portrait as a Forest in a Wildfire 50

TABLE OF CONTENTS

IV.

In the Woods 55
Lotus 56
On Becoming 57
Breathless Autumn 58
Portrait of the Sun on a Woman 59
Strawberries 60
First Fig 61
There's a delta 62
Peter and Ralph Waldo Emerson Walk through the Woods Together 64
Babysitting 66

V.

Family Creche 71
How to Prevent Ice Crystal Formation in Your Heart 72
Reflection 73
Where 74
Delilah 75
Telling Stories 76
After the Psalms Have Ended 77
One and Two Star Reviews of Fenian's Irish Pub, Jackson, MS 78
Cat and Roach 79
Not Yet Home 80
On the Anniversary of Mother's Death 81
Autumn in Mississippi 82

VI.

Capitalism 87
Rebellion 88
Wingless Flight 89
Self Portrait as Judas 90
Single 91
Moses and Zipporah Attend a Roller Derby Game 92
Janet Vaughan Refuses Failure 94
This Moment 95
I take care of myself, but the people around me don't 96

KNOCK-OFF MONARCH

Acknowledgements

Special thanks to the following journals for publishing these poems first, some in earlier forms:

"Vashti" and "Self-Portrait in Philadelphia" in *Badlands Literary Journal*

"Bedroom" (published with a different title 'Writing around the self') and "Ketoacidosis" in *Jet Fuel Review*

"Breathless Autumn" in *Southword Journal Online*

"First Fig" in *Drunk Monkeys*

"Naming," "Only," "On my drive home from the east coast," "In the grocery store parking lot," "Notes on an Afternoon Train," and "How to Prevent the Formation of Ice Crystals in Your Heart" in *isacoustic**

"Moses and Zipporah Attend a Roller Derby Game," in *Sport Literate*

"Transformation" in *Occulum*

Special thanks also to the following for their support and encouragement: Jennifer L. Knox, Debra Marquart, Matty Layne Glasgow, Michael Nyers, Kate Wright, Mike Robbins, Keygan Sands, Kartika Budhwar, Brendan Curtin, Chloe Clark, Jessica Winchell, Eileen Forsyth, Ashley Bleicher, Donna Spruijt-Metz, Craig Dinwoodie, AK, Dana Bridges, Dana Eckstein, Ian Arturo, Anna Stolarski, Brittany McLean, Rebecca Ferlotti, Tasha Layton, Mike Dockins, Renee Christopher, Amalie Kwassman, and countless others who listened, offered suggestions for possible futures and ultimately believed in my work. Without your assistance, this wouldn't have been possible.

Crystal Stone

I

KNOCK-OFF MONARCH

First Impressions

The girl who sat down next to me on the bus smells like a hot-dog-gas-station-soda burp. If I'd seen her from the glass, I would've imagined Tresemmé, L'Oréal, maybe a Sephora concealer. Now I'm looking for the ugly orange price sticker on her bookbag. She's clean. On the outside, me too. I smell like Victoria's Secret bombshell; I wear the perfume every morning. I bet she doesn't look at me and know my first bed had netting to keep cockroaches out. I bet she can't tell mom died in her shit, drunk. A few months ago, I met a classmate in the park. "You Jewish?" she asked. I'm not, but I get it. I grew up on the east coast, too. "We're American," my Poppy told me every time I asked about our ancestry. "Gesundheit," he told me every time I sneezed. When I taught children in the Mississippi delta, they didn't understand my hair. "What kind of mix you is?" I didn't know how to answer. When another student finally asked me, "What kind of not-straight are you?" I looked dumb, too. Black men tell me I'm thick for a white girl. When an Indian friend noticed my dad's skin tone for the first time, she laughed, "Somebody in your family did something they shouldn't have!" The family jokes that he's the neighborhood 'Mexican lawn service' because even in his fifties with two metal knees, a metal disc in his back and a metal hip, he landscapes for extra cash. I first admitted I was queer to a black woman. She told me I twisted Jesus' words when I close-read the Bible for her and barely spoke to me again. The first girl who reminded me I was straight looked white, but wasn't. She told me she wouldn't shower after resting in my bed because she smelled like me. I would've given her the rest of the laundry detergent if it meant I wouldn't hear from her again. My sheets weren't my scent anyway: they smelled like my ex-boyfriend who climbed trees in cowboy boots and told me he imagined I would be more sultry in his thick southern drawl. Both the man I loved and the woman I never would were mixed: half-European, half-Middle Eastern. A boyish girl I met is in the fourth grade. She's short and straight. She opens the cork to a bottle of shaved color. She tells me, "I like the smell of crayons. It's my scent." This doesn't surprise me at all. I expected that.

Crystal Stone

Knock-Off Monarch

On my drive home,

the trees are walking towards me,
through me. In this cold, my skin is

a mandala of veins. A barbed wire
fence next to me is braided

with trash. My dad says, *build
a wall, build a wall.* The pavement

is black sand and the sharks washed
ashore from cold shock look up at me.

I know those eyes. They are not living
mirrors. They are not fountains flowing

and water isn't wet when it's ice.

Crystal Stone

Knock-Off Monarch

Only

The lawnmower. The mid-afternoon shade.

From my window, the shine of leaves. I hear God
called Moses from the bushes. In front of my house

only stone. Moses looked away. I dare God to show
his face. I've looked all over: the bottom of cereal

boxes, the ice cream truck window, mother's jewelry
box, my lover's eyes, a tailgate under the stars.

I blew on every dandelion I found in the grass.
The seeds stuck to my hair and I only heard

my own voice. *Be patient.* I don't want to be
stung by a hornet waiting. At the Episcopal church

on Sunday, most of the hair is white if there's hair
at all. God's people are aging. Do we get closer

to death only when we get closer to God? When people
say to *take care* what they really mean is *go away.* I can't

touch the sidewalk without breaking a grasshopper's back.

Crystal Stone

Knock-Off Monarch

God is

not an octopus   in the Mediterranean   he's like a jellyfish
that outlives children   who do not know yet   to be reborn
what goes through its mind   when cells converge in the water
with no family but what he created   god lifts his hand to drink
water   the sun goes rogue   in one of his towns   he stopped
leaving his kingdom   a few months back   trapped in an ocean
he ran out of ink when he made me   watched me wander
down the street   four years old   with just a dog by my side
he causes others, too,   neighbors sick, dying   to pay bills
always   working long hours god grows   tired of it all
what if he made less   elements to react and explode   what if he
never made life   just decorations maybe   video games
there would be no suffering   no need   the jellyfish
attaches himself to a boat   he wants to explore the Atlantic
the waters are much colder   god takes a shower
wishes to start over but he can't   go anywhere his reputation
is unknown   the jellyfish doesn't recognize his kinds
they are taking over the waters   god sees   his reflection
they are all thousands of years old   what a shame to live
forever   with the same face

Knock-Off Monarch

Against Faith

We build robots with forks
because there are no
screwdrivers. I am not

a madwoman in the tongs.
Sadness is not breakfast.
The robot is an aimless

spider. The fork was left in
the rocks below my window.
A woman wakes me singing

gospel passing by at 3 am. *Until
the day I die,* singing. Everything
new is bills. I'm not building

anymore, I don't care.
Motion needs no engine.
Sadness comes without beckon.

All winners eventually cheat.

Crystal Stone

21

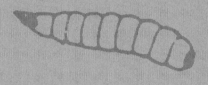

Knock-Off Monarch

Noah Goes to Rehab

The earth wasn't all that flooded. His wife
tired of cleaning the carpet, sink, and toilet
every Saturday, the Sabbath, when she was
supposed to rest. "It's me or that," she said
in a typical wifely way. Always an ultimatum,
but this time, she meant it. His dirty clothes,
his orange-bristled toothbrush and the pine sol
were street-side waiting for his collection.
She handed him the papers, changed the locks,
made windmills out of his bottles of Smirnoff.
He wasn't an all or nothing guy: he knew moderation
in other areas. Only two of each kind. Only two
of each shot would be enough, he imagined.
One more chance, he was warned. It was a lot of pressure
but he tried. They survived a year of ark-living.
It would be a shame to give it up for this.
He spent the whole month sober, missing the taste
of water after his fifth shot. Water was just water
now. His wife was so happy when he came back
grumbling. She made his favorite foods three meals
a day for two weeks before she fatigued, bored.
She missed going out with her friends. "I'll be back,"
she said. He let her go. Watched the way her hips
swayed like a mug of stout, sloshing, sashaying,
warm from the sun on the roof of the beer garden.

Crystal Stone

KNOCK-OFF MONARCH

Drawing Mother

When mother first took her screwdriver
from the bottom drawer, I drew

her cheeks pink, like flamingo wings
the way they got when I ruffled her

feathers. I drew her brown hair wavy;
her nose, long and full: a proper German

look. I never showed how her face grew
wrinkly like the parachute pants or how

her brows furrowed like Spanish accents
on vowels once visibly drunk. I only

fought to stay at home when she asked
me to leave with her. When I lost the battle,

I walked to the car with the crayons
and paper still in my hands. In the door's

handle, the crayons melted. In my mouth,
some juice. In mom's mouth, the aftertaste.

Crystal Stone

Knock-Off Monarch

Naming

      We point, trying to distinguish
the shape of the stratus:

      That cloud is voluptuous.
Those hairpin curls

      electrify the vast. With such hips,
it dares us to want. That cloud is

      a prostitute. Do you see the way
it sashays through the blue,

      as if the owner? But this cloud is an
object, bottle-neck length

      reaching upward—its face beyond
the frame of the sky.

      This cloud is a parent. In the wind,
it breaks apart into nothing

      but rain.

Crystal Stone

KNOCK-OFF MONARCH

In the Living Room

A bird sees its reflection in the window.

The thud when it falls is the sound we all make when we get close
to the truth of ourselves.

We still see color when our eyes are closed, but the shapes aren't
regular polygons.

A window is a regular polygon, but the molecules of skin are not.

I feather my words a skin of window or truth.

When I see myself, I don't recognize beyond.

There is bird poop suspended in the air right above
my hair's edge.

Crystal Stone

Knock-Off Monarch

Nevertheless, Jochebed* thought

about being a suicide or a sommelier.
A grave digger or a beer brewer.
A necrophiliac or an aphrodisiac.
At the grocery store, the aisles were
all *buy one, get one free.* Some of this,
none of that. She stopped shopping
because she liked it. She stopped
crocheting because she needed sweaters.
She said goodbye because she loved. Too
much. The sky. The dirt. The stink bug.
The soup. At dinner, the air was all save-
room-for-dessert. The champagne-cork
bruised breath. The tongue stemmed and
tied. The aroma flesh tomatoes saliva
skunk. She stopped eating because she
was hungry. None of that, none of that.

Jochebed is the mother of Moses in the Bible.

Crystal Stone

KNOCK-OFF MONARCH

Before the News

We think we've seen it all: the stars
dying in the butterfly nebula, the milky

stains on the child's lip when she washes
the cookie down, the strange sea cucumber

on a National Geographic feature. The lady
bugs in the corner of the room don't bite

us in our sleep. One day, we discover the stars
aren't all that's dying. The cookies aren't

the only secrets in the child's mouth. In anger,
we throw words and miss the poems.

Our pictures forget the sun. Just because
we have fingertips. We don't always touch.

Crystal Stone

Knock-Off Monarch

House Keys

after CD Wright

the lullaby	the prayers	the candles
the recorder	the tapes	the deception
the judge	the custody	the drawer
the bottle	the drive	the secret
the pizza	the flight	the floor
the shame	the exit	the hush
the blue	the police	the vacation
the motel	the vomit	the lullaby
the husband	the grass	the hand
the fireplace	the absence	the call
the bed	the body	the question
the escape	the house	the curtains
the lock	the locking	the locked

Crystal Stone

Knock-Off Monarch

Poverty

In the dream, I am petting
geese. The road is paved

in droppings. My feet are
greener. In the dream, I can

leave whenever I like. I want
to stay. When I sip the water,

I witness a four-leaf clover
grows from the drain. I don't

take the luck. I don't need
to. The pennies I'm rubbing

become the sun and there's heat
in the house. I am a genie.

I rub the tea kettle to let
my hair hang tea bags.

My eyes breathe rooibos
steam. I can handle the snow

pavings when they come, the white
sting of socks or whatever I use

to warm me. The aged rum
I've left on the bar unfinished.

The blue copper light. The dead
blisters drying between my toes.

Crystal Stone

Knock-Off Monarch

One and Two Star Reviews of Storybook Land,
Egg Harbor Township, New Jersey
a found poem, after Aimee Nezhukumatathil

Looked like there would usually be a small pond, but the water
was drained.

We were on the train, in the front seat, when the gasoline
literally exploded. Thank god I covered my 8-month old.
The poor girl who worked there got gasoline in her eyes
and didn't even have anything to wash them out with.
Not sure I'm coming back.

There was a sheep whose coat was matted and overgrown.

Dirty, expensive and too babyish.

I called and asked if I showed our stamps and receipt, if we
could come back. They told me no refunds. I didn't ask for a refund.
My daughter is heartbroken.

outdated, needs upgrading.
they are racist and rude.

They had a Mother Goose exhibit where there wasn't enough room
for three geese.

It isn't the best, but it isn't the worst.

The birds were rolling in the dust to stay cool.

Crystal Stone

Knock-Off Monarch

Kitchen
after Eduardo Corral

Instead of vased flowers, a cactus.
Instead of an oven, a cabinet

for bread. Instead of water, vodka.
Instead of a spatula, a belt.

Instead of conversation, comic strips
from Sunday papers on the counter.

Instead of granite, yellow. Instead of prayer,
silence. Instead of dinner, a nap.

Instead of a mother, a six year old girl
learning to cook for a younger boy.

Crystal Stone

My Family As Disciples at the Last Supper

Peter pushes his plate away from him. His brother, Andrew, doesn't notice. Andrew is busy avoiding the texture inside the lima beans. He swallows them like pills, one at a time. Mary Magdalene is temperamental, too. "Andrew, just eat them," she says impatient. "And Peter," She pauses for a beat, smears her hand across his plate and wipes the potatoes on his nose. "Does this look clean to you?!" Judas also wears his dinner. In his beard, framing a throaty laugh. Jesus, too. *How good it is we're all together.* Thomas doesn't hear Jesus' thoughts. He rolls his eyes, offers to help Mary instead. Andrew offers his opinions about everything but the beans: oil browned the eel to perfection. Too much salt on the potatoes. The apricot tastes perfect. Jesus doesn't notice, deep in thought. He wants to make a speech, but he questions himself. *Am I sober enough?* The twins of Zebedee bicker. One of them farted. *Is it the right time?* He questions his company. *Tomorrow is my last day,* he says as he sets the wine glass down. He taps it with his fork like he would make a toast. It chips, but everyone stops to hear him. *What do you call wine spilled for many?* He makes a joke, instead of a parable. He never shares the punchline. Why talk about death in this moment, wine-drunk together, their plates so close to being clean?

Crystal Stone

35

Knock-Off Monarch

Mom interrupts Solomon

"Do you want to be the diaper changing
lady for the rest of your life?" She asked
him, arms crossed, drunk. Solomon
didn't look up to her again, not this time.
"Well?" mother was expectant. I watched
earnestly, expecting another version
of Ecclesiastes. How "all is vanity" because it'll be
left to someone else. How we don't get to enjoy
what we make. He left the room. I followed
slowly. He chopped onions on a thin blue
board. The tears of the knife were mirrors.
He saw me. Still, he said nothing. I said,
"If I had a mother like yours, I'd be wiser."
He cut the tomatoes first, then the cilantro
in chunks, each looking like four leaf clovers. "Dead
flies give food a bad smell . " he said, garlic
between his fingers, cut in wedges. Boiled,
water almost ready, I assured him, "Don't
worry, our roaches are odorless." Whether he
believed me or not, he didn't open the cupboard.
He didn't need it. His palace had fresh herbs,
vegetables. It was only by his kindness we ate.

Knock-Off Monarch

Ketoacidosis

With trash hammer-sloshed across the floor,
the house burps stale people-breath
where there are no husband tears, moans—
young eyes look-look away.

The house burps stale people-breath
while the officer's radio buzzes.
Young eyes look-look away—
virgin-unvirgin body in yellow-rum sheets.

While she buzzed, the officer radios.
The husband watched silently, skin as mead—
virgin-unvirgin body in yellow-rum sheets.
Will he sound-sleep in their bed?

The mead watched silently, husband just skin;
officers collect bottles, evidence—wondering,
will he sound-sleep in their bed?
Second wife now gone, lying in her waste.

Officers collect bottles, evidence. I wonder:
where are the husband tears, moans—
second wife gone, lying in her waste
with trash hammer-sloshed across the floor?

Crystal Stone

37

III

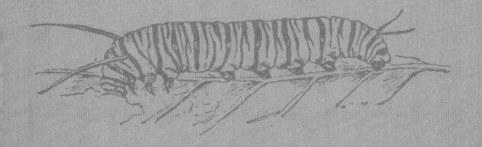

Knock-Off Monarch

Promise

My next poem will sound like someone else.
It will be brave, change someone's mind
about poverty. My next poem will be a recipe:
I'll teach 'em how to cook daddy's squirrel
potpie, rub pork ribs the right way,
mash potatoes like a man and baconwrap
their vegetables tight. My next poem
will be skinny from smoking: a backyard
barbeque, some prayer candles and maybe
a firecracker or two. My next poem will
be patriotic: there will be guns in it, because
how else will it defend itself? My next poem
will destroy, fire wrongly, and kill a child.
My next poem will stand for brotherly love,
Philadelphia, like it belongs there. It'll say
hoagies and *jimmies* and *freedom*. It will
reek of Yuengling, stumble through South Street,
steal Thanksgiving turkeys and eat bass
right out the Schuylkill. My next poem will be
a home-wrecker: the worst kind ever seen.

Crystal Stone

KNOCK-OFF MONARCH

Vashti

Pulling back the curtains, she notices
the flowers. Today, dewdrops on the petals
shine like crystals of the royal crown.
The flowers tell her it's vogue to run away.
She catches herself, falling from
flower-words or wine-nausea.
We would leave, too, if we could —
She did not sleep that night, woke up
in sweats. Plucked the flowers. Orphaned
them in cold water by the window.
The next morning, there was no dew,
no voices from the curtains she could hear.
The king called her, but could not find her—
only the translucent, petal-frail sheet
of skin once wearing the crown.

Crystal Stone

KNOCK-OFF MONARCH

Bedroom

There's a picture on the wall:
a woman whose breast almost exposed
winks a sure glance at a man behind her.
He looks like he's going to kiss her.

The walls are green, though. The draft
sighs, as if he knows it—knows the ending.
But there is no ending or resolution,
just the objects of an in-use room:

the unemptied can of white trash.
A hamper of dirty laundry. Creased
pillows. A ticking clock on a wooden desk.
Outside the window, the base of the beech

tree looks like an elephant foot, stepping
unbalanced—like the picture-woman.
From the corner, a cello watches silently,
brown-nosing, strings long out of tune.

Crystal Stone

KNOCK-OFF MONARCH

Describing Memory

Dunes wrinkle a river valley on Mars,
but there is no water. My car is sandy

from shells found at Mexico Beach
two years ago. Now farther away, I don't

try to hear the ocean. I drink water
from the faucet even when it is orange.

It hasn't hurt me yet: not the sulfur or lead,
not the silence or distance. I still use

my sink and car every day. I don't remember
the water until a visitor's ear listens for waves.

Crystal Stone

KNOCK-OFF MONARCH

Self-Portrait in Philadelphia

At my feet, trash grows from
the ground like wildflowers.
Beside me, windows act as mirrors
that remind me of the Schuylkill.
I can see signs of aging:
swelling in the river's center,
sunspots on its wrinkling surface.
I imagine bass and perch below drinking
mercury, barium and arsenic.
What does it taste like, I ask
the river that unrolls like a tongue.
But it has lost its sense of taste,
become mute—In the wind,
there may be a whimper or cry
silenced by on-going traffic, but
I cannot hear it. I do not notice
landscapes that came before, or know
how the river glowed in its youth.
I just kick stones and trash aside,
wondering if anything below
the sidewalk waits to bloom.

Crystal Stone

45

Knock-Off Monarch

In the grocery store parking lot,

the sugared sky powders
the nose of the child who asks

for more than his mother has to offer.
Her tampons look like candy.

They are not pop rocks and the cotton
is dry on the tongue. The mother

does not frown. What's one more
missing piece? Her son is a breath of fresh

menthol smoke. She doesn't realize
the slow blackening of lungs,

how her lips and skin are greying,
or that this moment—her son's arms

in her worn leather bag, cotton strings
hanging out the mouth with a tongue

that spits and begs for water—will happen
again. Next time, he will leave her, arms

outstretched, digging for candy,
someone else's cotton on the tongue.

Crystal Stone

KNOCK-OFF MONARCH

Notes on an Afternoon Train

I am stuck between a couple:
the boy closes his eyes while his
girlfriend feeds him over my head.

*

I can see my body better than
theirs in the dim of the station.
My face in the glass is wrinkled.

*

The boy's bike next to my legs
makes it hard to reach for the pole,
hold on and read while in motion.

*

A coffee is spilled. The liquid
branches out like long fingers
trying to touch my bare toes.

*

The blue of the train is not like
sky. It is a speckle of blue jay,
but has no song, just screech.

Crystal Stone

47

KNOCK-OFF MONARCH

Surrender
after Linda Gregg

Every day starts and ends the same
except when it doesn't: today,
few cars or people pass. No need:
this bridge leads almost nowhere.
Cornfields stretch for miles
beyond. I watch night drop
behind the trees: an old habit.
Light divides being from absence.
Mayflies rise like church-goers
to the sounds of cricket choirs.
I am unfaithful. I remember
how people said God's harmless
when he's answering prayers.
But I've never seen good come
from anybody knowing everything.
Streetlights are waking and they
hold back the moon brass with rust.
Let the water below run black. Let web.
Let the spider. Let land. Let light.
Let trees stretch out. Let be. Let sing.

Crystal Stone

Knock-Off Monarch

Transformation
  after Cattelan's *Bidibidobidiboo*

The squirrel is dead   hair down   the gun at his feet
glossy, the room   white   when I was in Jamaica a white
girl said   "the children dream   of coming to America"
I said the squirrels   are missing   the kids tell me
they're at the zoo   the squirrels at home   run in the streets
sometimes the trees   sometimes my pot-pie   little grey
hairs   stick out the crust   in texas   I was snow
white and fed   the squirrels   my bagels   they were fat
with yellow bellies   when I lived in Mississippi   there were
lizards   in the bathtub   I stopped thinking
about squirrels   I had no kitchen table just dirty dishes, but
I ate spinach quesadillas   with organic salsa   I don't
remember the texture   of squirrel tendons   between my teeth
or the skin of squirrel   in my basement   but I've been
this squirrel   head down on the table   wishing the papers
on the floor   metallic wrinkles that could straighten my hair
slick with grease   I'd sip   my half-empty shot glass
and I'd be   self-reliant   the dream

Crystal Stone

KNOCK-OFF MONARCH

Self-Portrait as a Forest in a Wildfire

These days, the fire inhales
the autumn tree confetti cake

it was given. There were other
birthdays: where the wind was

bellows for bark, the char smoothing
its edges after the burn. The clouds

moved so fast. The forking
veins from the leaves' midribs,

the spooning top of the mushroom's
body, the knife of a running fox.

How quickly it could all be
consumed. I was in a staring contest

with what I thought was a crescent
fungal moon, or maybe a tiny cloud

of smoke left from the oven that made
this evening. Before I knew, I blinked.

Crystal Stone

IV

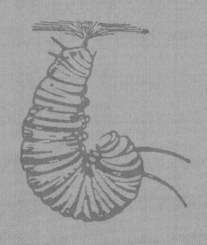

Knock-Off Monarch

In the Woods

i.

By the sycamore tree, I orphan my poetry alphabet soup.

The radio beside me says the nose gets colder when the mind works harder.

"Does thinking about the nose make the nose colder?" the squirrel's nose asks the deer's.

Above our head, the aphasiac clouds are warm.

ii.

The clover mite thinks it can doula words without voice.

It walks on the page of my book instead of the grass.

I smear the body on my finger. It looks like red pencil lead.

Could an ant recognize the antennae?

There are many in the dirt, but they stay in their mound.

iii.

The tree surrogates poetry, deer.

The deer remind me that people wander off.

The sky is not upside down, but the clouds are a table of my scattered thoughts.

The mushroom is an abandoned spore.

The spore refuses the sun, asks me, "Is the brain a tongue of yours?"
I answer, "Like lavender grows in a field of velcro."

I am losing touch with the spores of myself.

Crystal Stone

Lotus
after Adam Zagajewski

At night, the wind hiccupped
between the lips of chestnut trees
and the sky freckled with stars.
Orion walked Sirius to the moon.
I waved, but didn't stop to say hello.
By day, the sun stung like birth.
It was August, the day I met you.
Brown just the color of chai
swallowed with sugar at sunrise.
Nothing seemed different: the little
dipper still scooped up sky.
Thrush songs didn't change octaves.
Since then, I've learned that love
can't be found in songs or precious
stones, in ancient art, magic or church,
but only in these: earth and air,
ordinary silence. The ground may
grow a full garden, but with hands
together palms up, a single flower.

Crystal Stone

Knock-Off Monarch

On Becoming

I prayed for boobs every day until I got them. Men stopped looking at my eyes. They are too small and brown.

Some men tell me they like brown eyes, they just don't love me.

If smell was sonic, whiskey skin could cello deep sighs.

Morning sobers shock a hangover.

My eyes are broken levees, but the tears are not destruction.

The tears might be destruction.

The bigger the mess, the more satisfying the clean.

My mind is a coal field stripped bare. The lavender it grows is the love I think I can still give.

My heart fancies itself a dandelion and blows wishes.

The seeds spam the landfill. I am not the landfill. I am always the trash.

I am an earthy mosaic of dried and seeds, the sweaty ground.

If I was a cup of tea, the leaves would be unclothed and float.

Crystal Stone

Knock-Off Monarch

Breathless Autumn
after Joy Katz

The Wright brothers staked out a deserted beach in autumn
where their glider-kite dropped from nearby trees in wind.
Pegasus was still trying to jump over the moon
when Squanto's wife was canoeing with her children.
The Mayflower's name is misleading. Mums were blooming
when it arrived at the rock and the passengers realized
they didn't know a thing about fish or food in this new land.
Rosalind Franklin stayed inside, lab-coat white, preparing
data to be stolen (accidentally) the following year and
Watson's partner Crick drank apple cider in his yellow sweater
bragging that he knew "the secret to life".
Marie Curie, when she was born, looked into the future—
orange leaf-print in the window. The faint blue of waning day.
Remember the morning after, when George Washington
slept in with his wife at a hotel in Virginia?
Or how the groundhogs hibernated through days of harvest?
I became insane, Poe wrote, beneath a cheap reading lamp.
Students at a nearby university thought they had no stories to tell,
but Buffalo Bill didn't feel the same. He traveled the plains,
show-stage in tow, giving America a taste of the real Wild West.
Turkeys in a November woods felt safe—now rest
gobble-stopped on families' Thanksgiving spreads.
The truth is not for all men, Ayn Rand rolled her eyes
and put out her cigarette at the sight of her own blackened lungs.
Crazy Horse smoked tobacco until he died, when the leaves were yellow-green
but his daughter had no chance to miss him.
God punished Eve for apple-breath after a walk in a fruitful orchard.
By the firelight, Western children now form a ring-around-a-rosie
forgetting the autumn cries of the black plague or the one—it was almost December—
when Zagajewski questioned the season. What is its origin? he asked.
Why should it destroy dreams, arbors, memories? Breathless autumn.

Crystal Stone

Knock-Off Monarch

Portrait of the Sun on a Woman

her hair autumns from brown   to blonde halos
half-rainbows contour   the skin ridges
on her forehead   from laughing   or is it
choking? the sun   gazes brown
spots on the surface   the woman doesn't
notice, goes about   her day   like sun is
the accessory   she notices   the shadows of
her lashes are   raining   cloudy, grey   lips
are flooding   where is gold   where is
heat   she's forgotten the color   of her eyes
when she looks   down   she sees   the ends
of her hair   have stopped   shining
unravels,   splitting into fourths

Crystal Stone

Knock-Off Monarch

Strawberries

I
like
them
best
when

they shrivel up:

red bodies dusking dark purple and soft seeds
winter mouthed, used. They could've stayed in the garden, gone
under the ground, I could have stayed home, but they like the warmth
of my belly now, all twenty-four of them. Some days, I'm not hungry. I eat other

things instead. Lips occasionally, hair regularly, teeth almost never — the first boy
I kissed chipped his front tooth. He lived on a farm with a barn   full of rabbits
and a tarantula I avoided   when I could. He married the girl he left   for me

when I was thirteen.   Ten years later, married men still talk to me when
their wives are out: I just say no   every time,   my body makes me
lonely,   it's what people want from me.   Poetry, they say,
I know what they mean.   The strawberries also siren

men before they age out   of taste buds. I love
them best purple   from a long-life lived
on a green vine by much sunshine, not
nourished   with the lead-sulfur

water I brush   my teeth in
that shrivel grey my skin
lungs hair liver
soul.

Crystal Stone

Knock-Off Monarch

First Fig

I had never seen one outside a cookie.
When she handed it to me, brown and
bulbous like an onion, I didn't expect
it to juice with perfume at first taste.
A kiss from the pink mouth of a flower
grown inward. If the crunch it made
between my teeth was a wasp, I didn't
know. There were no wings or antennae
I could see. Just seeds, velvet skin.
A stem to throw away.

Crystal Stone

Knock-Off Monarch

There's a delta

juke joint and casino

in every blue eye I meet.

It's a gamble

and Robert Johnson riff, improvised

Blues — the thousand dollar

art I found

when I walked through

the shattered glass

window of an abandoned

furniture store on Farrish Street.

A homeless

man asked me for cigarettes,

then if I was scared

because the man I was with

had hurried away.

I wasn't but I didn't have

any cigarettes.

He was kind,

Crystal Stone

KNOCK-OFF MONARCH

told me if he wanted something,

he would just ask.

I moved on to the next

building with a blanket

and used needle. Now, I am

nine hundred miles away

looking into new blue eyes, searching

for the last.

My mom always asked

why I couldn't be happy.

When I try to make him

happy, he tells me

we will never be that.

I will never have blue eyes

but I've always seen

the brown

reflected back

in someone else's blue.

Crystal Stone

Knock-Off Monarch

Peter and Ralph Waldo Emerson Walk through the Woods Together

Peter says, "I've never seen this in Galilee."
He holds the poison ivy leaf upside down,
brings it to his nose to sniff. "Pain is superficial,"

RW says after explaining what would come
in the morning when Peter awoke from his dreams
of the honeysuckle RW handed him

for the first time this day. "It's so cold here,
even for autumn," RW nods. "Massachusetts seems
fickle," Peter continues. They didn't argue about

his correctness. They continued to forage mushrooms
and berries, misstep on vines, scare deer who lived
in the brush they cleared. After hours of near solitude,

they breaked for granola bars on red rocks overlooking a hill.
"You know," RW reminds him, "The torments
of martyrdom are most keenly felt by the bystanders."

Peter himself felt little pain the day he was murdered—
just the nails that broke his bones and the blood
that rushed to his head as his hair combed the dirt.

His brother Andrew stopped fishing and asked
Jesus again, this time in prayer, "what good is
this for many?" His mother never drank wine

again, retired her fine dresses and silks. *The only
thing grief has taught me to know is
how shallow it is.* RW thinks what Jesus didn't.

Crystal Stone

KNOCK-OFF MONARCH

Ever tell Jonah or Peter or Andrew or the nameless
mother: life is not eternal because we live forever
in the kingdom, but because the trees, the rocks,

the ocean never leave or sway because we're gone.
"All loss, all pain, is particular; the universe remains
to the heart unhurt." RW looks at the harvest moon,

so orange, so cratered, so untouched by human life.

Crystal Stone

Knock-Off Monarch

Babysitting

I wish I had the orange mascara of the trees
or the luster of the monarch's wings. Instead,

I have an apricot of rust on my fender. One
child told me I had the worst car he'd ever seen.

Another couldn't believe anyone ever thought
I was beautiful. I'm sure they're right about all

of it: children always tell us the truth we're not
willing to admit. One girl stole a dandelion

from my hand and crushed the seeds between
her fingers. She told me that she doesn't care

to see people make wishes that won't come true.
Another day, a boy tells me it's more fun

to want than to have. I agree: better to want
the man that could hold me than have him

hold another woman a few months later.
Better to want children than to hear them say

your love wasn't enough. Better to have nothing
but thoughts you can control, dreams like trees

more brilliant against the grey of clouds that
thunder, keeping me all day inside the house.

Crystal Stone

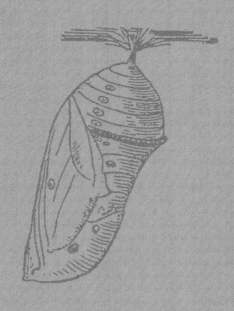

Family Creche

Baby
sits on a porch in a stable
The hay is itchy, but he does not cry. His mother is standing near,
hands outstretched. The sheep pay him no mind. Neither do I. Inside my mother sleeps

```
dead          in her waste                    at              the inn,
there is no room for Baby.                    young         children's
prayers            of                         wishing    to       be
Stars   of    Bethlehem                       distracts        angels.
I   want   to   ask   why.                    Was there no room   for
new               bills?                      Baby            Jesus
sleeps  when  I   knock                       at the door.      I am
too late.     Her body is                     gone.     In the absence,
a   boxed   offering—                         no spices,  frankincense
or myrrh.         Just                        her          old poems
wedding   rings   and        ashes           bow-tied in a  white case
Now   the   baby's   face   (young, newborn)  looks ashen.  I realize it's
just    porch    light      and the smoke of  my            neighbor's
chimneys.   They notice no   savior—          just the whisper of winds
reciting     ~~maybe a poem~~─────────────────~~prayer~~ nothing, like usual
```

Crystal Stone

KNOCK-OFF MONARCH

How to Prevent Ice Crystal Formation in Your Heart

Play dead, let the water leave you.
Sun will eventually thaw your bones.
When that happens, just find water
quickly. Most of us die
when our bodies are more than half-empty
of water. Few live where they cannot
endure. Some live anyway. Look:
the wood frog does not breathe
when ice crystal puncture the tissues.
But it's not over for them, spring comes
back. And Jesus walked on water, not ice.
Maybe he is a spider, silver-bodied,
black legs extended shore-to-shore.
Maybe he is the icicle that stabs the wood
frog's heart. Less life, more space
for the holy? No, Antarctica is not a wasteland.
Look closer: even by freezing waters,
lice make a hat on the young seal's head.

Crystal Stone

Knock-Off Monarch

Reflection

For the first time, I notice the orange horizon
is crooked in the sunset my grandmother painted.

It took two years for me to see the sloped banks the deer
waited by. It took even longer for scientists to follow

the toothed skin catfish to the vertical horizon in Ecuador
where it climbs cave walls instead of waterfalls. They

observe its body is not colorless or blind. They find
no algae there for it to eat and wonder: could it travel

for fun or was it forced to go? Last week, the blue
horizon of Tampico was not crooked, but curved—

the rain brought fish in small bundles on umbrellas
and in plastic bags shoppers left open. Is it a miracle

or a bad omen to find the glassy-eyed fish looking
upwards in unsuspecting hands? Better fish falling

from the sky than the ground crumbling beneath you.
Better waterspouts on rivers than hurricanes on land.

On the banks of my grandmother's painting, the deer
considers water from the orange river. There are barely

any ripples. Its family is just fine. It doesn't know
somewhere else deer suffer, fish have left their homes

Crystal Stone

Knock-Off Monarch

Where

I pour whiskey in my lemonade
to make the lemonade taste better:
the warm-sweet sting of a day now gone.
The ocean pours sea life onto the sand.
A hermit crab hides his face in a doll
and his legs poke out the eyes. He pours
his heart into her empty mind. After
the hurricane, the clouds don't pour,
they spit rainbows out their fuzzy tongues,
prove that devastation can be beautiful.
My thoughts are pores leaking, the skin
of the past enlarged. If the book was not
solid, words would spill on the floor
and I'd splash letters under my toes.
My lover would hold me again, remind
me he dumped the whole bottle to save
my life. I want to be trapped in a portrait
of a place where the birds can't catcall me
from the trees. I won't be the porcupine.
I won't hurt anyone from my corner of the frame.
My body will be a porch and I will hold
my lover upright. I will hold the birds'
waste, the squashed bugs, the trash left behind.
I will be the wood scraped porous and
sponge together the tree, sky and stream.

Crystal Stone

74

Knock-Off Monarch

Delilah

His hair limp in my hands:
A body of water made still.
Holding the braids, I wonder

What it felt like to rip limbs
Of a lion, break chains: no matter
The obstacle, an almighty

There. Then, to wake one morning
not knowing it had changed, God gone.
These braids just ordinary hair?

Crystal Stone

Knock-Off Monarch

Telling Stories

I only had surgery twice. The first time my tooth was stubborn. They needed to chain it to my braces so it'd come in straight. The second time they cut the tissue between my upper lip and gum so my gums would stop receding. I should've had surgery on my foot, but I don't trust doctors. Every time my dad had something replaced, they broke his bones. Growing up, I only liked some heights. When my friends asked me to ride this roller coaster, I said I couldn't. I was afraid my eyelashes would fall out. I wasn't born with many. In high school I never learned German. My mother wanted me to. I didn't want to speak in our mother tongue. I didn't even want a mother. Rumpelstiltskin said, "Er risst sich entzwei." But not me, I won't do it. My dad walked in with a fishhook in his finger. I taught myself not to shiver in the ten below winds. I taught myself to keep my body still while my lips cracked a white-pink lake. Now, after the last surgery, my dad has to keep his tongue still because the doctors cut part of it out. I wonder if this is what happens when we always say no. Talk too loudly, speak truth in strong words what we heard all our lives. Do our tongues always grow tumors to rebel against the telling?

Crystal Stone

76

Knock-Off Monarch

After the Psalms Have Ended

The poem requests a new form.

The poem centipedes down the pipes
sweaty she might be squashed.

The poem coral snakes a fart
to intimidate. *I'm not average,* she

fights. The poem black spider-balloons
silk parachutes over farm fields,

haunts the grass and homes in cobwebs.
The poem eagles monogamy, even though

she sits alone for months at a time.
Sometimes, the poem ivys in poison

and her readers' eyes rash in tears.
The poem doesn't human hives,

or cough, vomit or shit in her pants.
The poem plastic bags the groceries.

Once discarded, she hangs around
the readers' necks, seeking an after-life

or revenge.

Crystal Stone

Knock-Off Monarch

One and Two Star Reviews of Fenian's Irish Pub, Jackson, MS
a found poem, after Aimee Nezhukumatathil

There was old lipstick on my beer glass. It was lukewarm
at best.

As an Irish pub, it's as flat as their beer!

Stuffy, old building.
Couldn't get past the dust.

If I was 20 lbs heavier, the stairs would've collapsed.

Authenticity was the bread pudding: a disappointment. It was cold
and dry.

It did, however, have what most Irish pubs "up nawth" have:

a floor slanting to the street.

Crystal Stone

Knock-Off Monarch

Cat and Roach

The cat chases the roach running
under a couch the cat's paw fits

under the belly rips one leg
the roach on his back legs waving

the cat watches the doorbell
doesn't ring no sound from the

TV no more beer I come down
from the back of the couch

I observed the cat play
rub the roaches belly at work

a boy asks if I like the smile
he draws a frowning moon laughing

maniacally I'm confused the ceiling fan
tilts the floor the sorry roach

has no more legs the cat ate them
I see them hanging from her mouth

the moonlight her eyes are neon
signs no vacancy the stars

hang in the corner of the window
skinny legs in a bowl a mouth the floor

Crystal Stone

Knock-Off Monarch

Not Yet Home

We clapped mosquito fog, covered
our drinks with bloody hands while
trucks sprayed the air. Our beers

and fried okra: a new insect grave.
We didn't know whose blood we drank,
if the condensation on the glass was our

sweat or the beer's. We didn't care.
The soap in the back of my car melted
into aspirin into band-aids into black

seats: everything I owned lying there.
I took it all out just weeks later,
at my first home, where I slept on the floor

and when my engine gave up on the side
of a Jackson street, five men stopped
to help. One gave me gas, another oil.

Someone checked the transmission,
another the battery. One just offered
lunch, jokes, a business card where I sent

a thank you. My car didn't run that day,
empty. Despite some kindness and care.
The loan. No oil, no power, no more travel.

Crystal Stone

Knock-Off Monarch

On the Anniversary of Mother's Death

I only visited the house three times after her death.
The first time the door opened, a toothless man
still living there. The second time I looked
for her ashes. I lost them. Instead, I found
locked doors and a letter addressed to me.
A family wanted to buy her house. My childhood
curtains still hung in the window: the noose of an era
ended. Now, I live on the wrong side of Fortification
in my own place. Jackson, Mississippi is boring
but there are perks: $395 for rent and free pets
in the cupboards. In the delta, I saw my first kangaroo
in a playpen behind the counter of a pawn shop.
On Sunday, the town's empty because the owners
like football and God. It's apparently the Sabbath
for both. I don't mind, because I have Jack
in the bathroom. I drink whiskey more often than she
drank rum, but I have more friends. I am growing into her,
wintering, the way I said I never would, the way we all do
when we age. I wonder if she would be alive if I loved her.

Crystal Stone

81

KNOCK-OFF MONARCH

Autumn in Mississippi

Outside, the crepe myrtles are black
with mold. The eyes of the floating log
stare apathetically: *I don't care enough
to hurt you,* they say and close. Above,
the clouds island together volcanic.
I talk to myself or god: am I still a child?
I storm and the clouds threaten to wash
away the summer feel of heat. Inside,
I'm asked to clean up the bodies
of the roaches I smeared on the counter.
I don't. A man on the radio says the plants
have more leaves than their roots can hold.
They are bending over, dying. I look outside
again. The cypress trees are tall with kudzu capes.
They are not superheroes, but ghosts.

Crystal Stone

VI

KNOCK-OFF MONARCH

"Capitalism"
after Tomaž Šalamun

"Capitalism"
you are a painted lady butterfly
a knock-off monarch
with brown and white blotched
wings. Charm me, I'm waiting.
I see you: on the goldenrod,
aster, blazing star, thistle,
and wind. Smoke me
a cigar, blow truth.

Crystal Stone

KNOCK-OFF MONARCH

Rebellion

Monday I'm afraid to fart in wine class
because the lesson is on aroma. I already
learned how to judge in church. *Did you hear*

Katie's mom gives her condoms?
The instructor says, "grapey," "foxy," "harvest"
but there's not wheat or rye here. No ergot.

We're not witchy or witching. We just sniff, sip,
and spit. *Leave as you came,* she warns.
This time only, *Smell.* I smell the glass,

face down off the rim. It smells like pencil lead,
even after I swirl. Maybe there's lead in the wine
just like there was in the water back there.

Like there was ergot in the wheat,
but they thought the bread was enchanted
and burned the women instead. Stake me

at the burning hollow. Or don't. Stop me
from washing my clothes in tea bags, baking
bread in garlic or smearing lime-blueberry

jam. I like my wheat and wood-fired ovens.
Without the women. With lots of butter. Wine
we can drink without foxy pineapple or grass.

Crystal Stone

Knock-Off Monarch

Wingless Flight

Even ions move. They are frustrated
lightning. So am I. When I was 14,
a woman I didn't know told me
there was a sweetness she couldn't place.
I was honey flowing from the stone.
I'm not that fluid. I'm a dry stone
kicked, that's how I wander.
Someone's always pushing me out.
Heat shifts ions, too, but they can sway
in their instability and more purposefully,
create an electric honeycomb.
Even ancient viruses in my DNA formed
proteins that told my fetal cells how to
differentiate. What gave them their out?
Perhaps mom's diet or my own
imperfect molecules. I guess everything
needs to feel like it matters. Little
lays at rest in the world undisturbed.
With the right force or roadblocks, even
what doesn't live can look like it breathes.

Crystal Stone

KNOCK-OFF MONARCH

Self-Portrait as Judas

My mother thought I'd be a girl. She had
a hunch. My dad thought he was resourceful

enough I'd always have a home. Growing up,
I was so clumsy I split a stink bug into three

when I stubbed my toe, farted in yoga when I tried
to downward dog. Dad pressed every button

on the dentist's chair before the dentist came
back. Dad wasn't worried about being discovered.

I never tried to do anything worth discovering.
I've only kept one secret. On the porch now,

after returning the money I earned, the painted
lady butterfly thinks my skin is the style

of dogbane or milkweed. He stays longer
than he should. It's not that I've never loved.

Even now, the cat sleeps in my shadow. I've been
outside for so long there are white spots in my tan.

But what did he lose, dying only to rise again?
When I kissed him and bought the graveyard, I gave

what I would never get back in return: a blameless after
noon. Gentle hands on the palm. A warm memory.

Crystal Stone

Knock-Off Monarch

Single

If I'm lucky, I won't marry a poet:
all their wandering—the tree
is an exclamation point. No, it is
a question mark, branches curve
like wanting. A body wanting?
They can never make up their minds.
The fish are plentiful and small,
they fall from the sky. Then, nothing.
No fish. No sky. No smallness.
Everything is grand: I could tell my partner
"When we forget, we don't know what we lost."
This would be a new poem. No, it'd be a new
series of poems about loss. There are
saints in it, too. Many saints and prophets.
Hindu gods and goddesses who came
to a feast and left presents. Then, extinct
sea life washes ashore or maybe mammals.
Suddenly, we're in a new poem again.
Another new poem. Another day on the couch
cuddling after work and I would wonder
what audiences and portraits he'd dream up.

Crystal Stone

Knock-Off Monarch

Moses and Zipporah Attend a Roller Derby Game

He and Zipporah drank brandy hot chocolates
and ate blueberries on the floor by the space heater.
It was winter. Zipporah was bored so she melted
pencils in the tea candle lights they had in the window
until Moses hid them from her. "Please," she asked.
"Can we go to the roller derby this time?"
He was always busy: extinguishing burning bushes,
delivering commandments to local courthouses, parting
the red sea, but when their own oven caught
flames, she had to take care of it herself—the wall
still scarred black from smoke. Moses didn't mind;
in his 96th year, appearances meant little to him.
His wife's love meant much more. "I will
give it a try tonight." He prefered the quiet
nights at home holding hands, but he saw the way
she rushed to change into something more festive
and knew it was the right time to buy tickets.
The sight was jarring: he had never known women
to be so violent—not even his wife who cheered
shamelessly as the visiting team's jammer took
a knee, struggling to get up after a large blow.
She daydreamed about wearing the star herself,
but she never had the courage to try. How
would it reflect on her husband if she took pleasure
taking and giving hits? Wearing fishnets in public?
The patterns on their tights resembled the sand
at the bottom of the red sea. If only she could part
with comfort, divinity, purpose and for a few hours
let the wheels roll her somewhere else, in circles,
where she wouldn't be a wife or a mother

Crystal Stone

Knock-Off Monarch

where god wouldn't be the announcer calling her
moves. She could pretend, for a minute, god wouldn't
know her every thought or desire, the knowledge
he possessed without her verbal consent. "If I were
a derby girl, my name would be zip-through-her."
She smiled, threw back her $1 beer. *How strange,*
Moses thought. *To love someone and never
know how much they might want something else.*

Crystal Stone

Knock-Off Monarch

Janet Vaughan Refuses Failure
after Rose George

*"What I hated most was people's acceptance: 'Yes, I have had seven children
and buried six, it was God's will.' I hated God's will with a burning hatred."
- Janet Vaughan, from Rose George's 'A Very Naughty Little Girl'*

Don't tell me that I cannot god—
she came to me, no veins
in her arms. Skin burned. My ice cream
truck housed the blood I would use
for her transfusion. There was no
jingle at her doorstep where I
stabbed her bone with the biggest
needle I could find. She lived.
Last time someone told me
my treatment was impossible,
I drank the liver extract myself.
Men were so embarrassed they could only
ask advice in letters. I didn't mind,
it wasn't the first time I was refused
lab mice and had to use street
pigeons instead. The skeletal men
in striped pajamas thought I was a Nazi
when I walked into the tomb
searching for the living among the dead.
I saved their lives if they let me
and sometimes when they didn't.
After I crouched low in the trenches,
visited the camps for months, hands-bloodied
with needles that threaded skin, I filled
the dumpsters: I could never eat
ice cream or don striped pants again.
In the lab, I would just hold
plutonium, hope I could discover
something else we might have
overlooked while so afraid to be wrong.

Crystal Stone

94

Knock-Off Monarch

This Moment

Samson had no eyes and a bald head
when God gave him the nod and strength

to kill himself. The columns came down
after Vesuvius erupted and fossilized

the bodies. Sometimes I'm so happy
I want to be covered in ash and laid

to rest beneath my maple tree or left
to rot roadside where bees could make

honey in my rib cage. Life is so sweet
at a standstill, in simple brushstrokes

on a painter's canvas. There the lion
looks like glitter, volume, and light.

Crystal Stone

KNOCK-OFF MONARCH

I take care of myself, but the people around me don't

notice. The girl across from me at the bar coughs
chunks onto my face. I wipe them off. She leaves
for the bathroom. The bartender informs me
his girlfriend lets him see other women so she won't have to

suck his dick. He over pours my drinks too often.
I let them water. I let myself sober. He touches
my back, invites my friends to come over. We did,
but the stories I could tell are just stories. That day,

the split lip I had for three weeks healed miraculously.
Before, I ate trail mix on the toilet while I bled
a cherried smile. Now I can laugh again. At myself
and the circumstances. I have what I need: I pulled

the filing cabinet out of the trash in high school.
The pantry from an open garage. Leaves from a sumac
tree I stuck in cardboard carpet tubes to make the backyard
look like a tropical beach with palm trees. They

were poisonous. I bathed in oatmeal for two weeks,
but all anyone else saw was the rash. And when the broken
pump spilled gas on the ground, the attendant gave me
a paper sno-cone cup and two paper towels to clean up

the mess. I used my hands instead. Now I steal my friend's
socks because it's been awhile since I heard from her.
She has a new boyfriend. He can buy her a new pair
for Christmas. I saw an Elf on the Shelf the first time

when I was in college. I convinced myself it was a drone
that flew around the house recording videos. My dad
laughed every day because of my anxiety. I never told
that story. "She's gullible," they all thought. So gullible.

Crystal Stone

96

© YVIE SOJKA

About the Author

A native of Pottstown, Pa., Crystal Stone's poetry has appeared in various international journals, including *Anomaly, Occulum, Driftwood Press, BONED, Eunoia Review, isacoustics, Tuck Magazine, Writers Resist, Drunk Monkeys, Coldnoon, Poets Reading the News, Jet Fuel Review, Sigma Tau Delta Rectangle, North Central Review, Badlands Review, Green Blotter, and Southword Journal Online.* In 2017, while earning an MFA from Iowa State University, she gave a TEDx talk called "The Transformative Power of Poetry." Crystal spends most of her free time writing poems while skating park trails in Ames, Iowa.

www.crystalbstone.com
www.instagram.com/stone.flowering
www.twitter.com/justlikeastone8